FEATHER PRESS

tender hearts club

Volume One
An Anthology of Love Poems
Edited by Ingrid Keir

Tender Hearts Club: Volume One
An Anthology of Love Poems

Copyright © 2026 by Feather Press

All rights reserved. No part of this book may be reproduced in any form or by any electronic or mechanical means, including information storage and retrieval systems, without permission in writing from the publisher, except by a reviewer who may quote brief passages in a review.

Copyrights to individual poems are retained by their respective authors.

Edited by Ingrid Keir
Cover design and interior design by Jennifer Barone

ISBN: 978-0-9979362-2-3

Published by Feather Press, Petaluma, CA
featherpressbooks.wordpress.com

Printed in the United States of America

For more information, please contact the publisher at: featherpressinfo@gmail.com

For Sierra,
my heart

tender hearts club

Introduction

Incantation // Ruth Crossman	10
Send Us // Norma Smith	11
Biography // Richard Stimac	12
In the Beginning // Elisa Salasin	14
The Only Museum I Want to Live In // Justin Demeter	16
New Constellation // Justin Demeter	18
3I/Atlas // Jennifer Barone	19
Even Though You're Not Here // Jennifer Barone	21
Illuminations // Gianmaria Franchini	22
Ciao, Stella Mattina // Anne Marie Wenzel	24
The Color of Rain: The Color of Sleep // Hollie Hardy	25
Ghazal on Fire // Hollie Hardy	27
Morning // Sara Biel	28
This Ordinary Morning Demanding Impossibles // E.K. Keith	30
Requiem to the Holy Mysteries // Peggy Morrison	32
Foreplay // Jeffrey Bryant	33
The Snack Bar at the Met // Jeffrey Bryant	34
I Need You Like Hydrogen Needs A Match // Bear	35
Breach // Val DeBarra	36
Marcus // Natasha Dennerstein	37
Green Space // Egan Reeve	38
Paloma // Luisa Guilianetti	40
Demeter // Luisa Guilianetti	42
Everything I Know About Love Fits Into This Monopoly Thimble // DJ Benhaim	44

Love Snores // Adrian Arias	47
New Birds // M.G. Martin	48
My Dragon // M.G. Martin	50
Hopelandic // Len Kuntz	51
Mount of Venus // James J. Siegel	52
My Mother Says // James J. Siegel	54
Dreamcatcher // K.R. Morrison	56
Motherland // Char Lacsina	57
Florida Clay // Victoria Dym	60
A Love Song for the City Before I Go // Joseph Voth	61
A Brief History of How the Heart Breaks // Joseph Voth	63
For My Husband Sleeping on the Floor Near Our Dying Dog // Michelle Patton	64
Between Two Raging Bulls // Michelle Patton	65
Tanta Paz: So Much Peace // Alexandria Giardino	66
Snow // Patrick Cahill	67
The Peach Fuzz on Your Knuckles // Lourdes Figueroa	68
Come Home // Lourdes Figueroa	69
Orchard of the Body // Brittiany Lema	71
Sweet Fruit // Candace Loheed	73
Bed 'n Breakfast // Al Averbach	74
Earthbound (don't come after me) // Shizue Seigel	75
There Are More Beautiful Things Than Aditya Roy Kapur // Elizabeth Shanaz	76
l o v v v e // Tom Batchelder	78
Tender Hearts Club // Ingrid Keir	79
Afterglow // Ingrid Keir	80
Things That Make You Remember Dreams // Kary Hess	82

Matrimony // Jonathan Siegel	83
Untitled // Lam Khong	86
Oh My love // Maggie La Rochelle	88
What Is Love? // Lynn Light	90
Six Pack // Elisabeth Nails	92
XXXmas 2025 // Phillip T. Nails	93
We Shall Call It Love // Brian Cronwell	96
Octavia // Maw Shein Win	99
Octavia // Maw Shein Win	100
By The Creek // Kim Shuck	101
Boxes // Heather Romero-Kornblum	102
Duplex // Kelechi Ubozoh	103
Confession // Genny Lim	107
Seal Song // Gail Mitchell	108
Cousin Kayla's Affair // Paul Corman Roberts	110
In The Company of Your Sweater // Karisma Rodriguez	112
Each Morning // Chelsea Wills	114
Contributor Bios	116
Acknowledgments	127
About Feather Press	128
About the Editor	129

Words of a Feather, Candace Loheed

Introduction

"We aren't bodies at all; who we are is the love inside us, and it is that love alone that determines our value."
— Marianne Williamson, *A Return to Love*

We are making this book now because the world is asking us—over and over—to harden. To look away. To shrink our circles of care. To treat love as private, sentimental, optional. In a time of rising cruelty, of borders drawn tighter, of care made conditional—love feels like the thing we're not supposed to have time for.

I don't believe that.

I believe love is powerful. I believe love is political. Not in the small sense of slogans, but in the living sense of how we choose to move through the world—what we protect, what we refuse, what we make room for, what we are willing to feel. Love is boundary-less in the way it insists on connection: to the body, to the earth, to community, to grief, to joy, to the complicated tenderness of being human.

This anthology gathers love in all its forms. Erotic love and everyday love. Revolutionary love and quiet love. The love that aches, that longs, that wallows. Love lost and love found. Love as an opening. Love as an ending. Love that is muddy and unclear, and love that arrives like a bell—clean and undeniable. Love that refuses to disappear, even when everything around us tries to numb.

Because love is what apathy cannot touch. Love is what hate has never understood.

Poetry is one of the places where love can still be spoken plainly—without apology, without performance, without being reduced to something small. These poems do not ask love to be easy. They let love be honest. They let it be messy and radiant and real. They allow the heart to tell the truth.

I made *Tender Hearts Club* because I want to lift up love in the world. I want to practice it, not as an idea, but as a devotion. This anthology is the first in a series—a sustained commitment to cultivate love and to show my daughter that it matters. That choosing compassion matters. That the heart is not a distraction from what's real—it is one of the most real things we have. The way we love shapes everything.

This book is a gathering. A small collective altar. A chorus of voices saying: we are still here, and we are still capable of tenderness. We are still capable of devotion. We are still capable of change.

May these poems remind you what you already know, somewhere deep in your body: love is not a soft afterthought. Love is a force. Love is a practice. Love is a way forward.

Welcome to the *Tender Hearts Club*.

Ingrid Keir
Editor, Feather Press

Incantation
Ruth Crossman

I bless you with precision
bless you with clean hands

bless the tools of your profession
bless your mind with swiftness

bless you with a steel mirror's strength
bless you with Sage and Juniper
bless you with Onyx and Jasper

bless you with protection
bless you with the sword of heaven
bless you with alchemy

bless you with ibogaine and mushrooms
bless you with bell hooks
bless you with transformation

bless you with space in dreams
bless you with roots sunk to earth
bless you with bare feet in sand

bless you with Ocean Beach at night
      the High Sierras and my mother's backyard full of bees

bless you with presence

Send Us
Norma Smith

Your love poems
The attachments
Come loose from their moorings

The ones who in decades past
Tried to feast
On your heart

Send them to us. We will
Print them
As they have imprinted themselves

On us. Their owners—
Their creators, their instigators—
Turn out

False in almost every case
The tender parts
Scattered across the room

That used to be
Home to us
They bleed

Flowing free
They dull our pain
Help us

Find other ways to describe
To our children
What was love

Biography
Richard Stimac

Our bodies contain histories, inheritances from infinite past generations, each meal eaten, each injury, illness, scar, or hardened callus, each night slept fitfully or at ease, each laugh, or cry, fretted for we were born, each act someone performed on us, each act we performed on ourselves. The days we live culminate in the blood and the bone we name the self. When we grant each other a touch of a hand, or a face, a back, a lips, of each crest and depression that structures the corpus of our lives, we read the uneven lines etched into the skin. Thus is the privilege of touch. For this, I have grown into gratitude.

Untitled, Kyle Knobel

In the Beginning
Elisa Salasin

in the beginning
he said:
*please never write
a poem about me*

now he texts:
i miss you
and I remember each morning
of our six months I got
g'day gorgeous
his pinged greeting

always uncapitalized
always made me smile

now I text:
i miss you too
& I do sometimes
miss his reverence
for the softness
of my middle-aged hips
I do sometimes
miss his many
lovely lowercased
intimacies

but this is not a poem
about him

this poem tells
of each strange
uncontrollable heart

seeking another

it tells of all
our searching
& aching

it tells of unknowable
equations that should
add up
to more

The Only Museum I Want to Live In
Justin Demeter

you enter a womb, watercolored amber glow
jackson-pollocked crack in the back
is patched with luna moths'
lacquered wings

when you stand inside our threshold
you can see slices of harvest
moon through open redwood beams

our attachment system is a creature
curled in the corner, animal
of brass and mirrors
placard beside them reads:

don't make eye contact, but do
feed them wildflowers

there's a broken typewriter melting
beside an antique sewing machine
she's humming *Dreams* while hemming
the last depths of me
I'm mending metal keys
while steadily pounding

poems like wild throats caught in chorus
the stillness of remembering
what you had
and what you lost

my canopy of knuckles stretches
over mid-October weather
and when it pours I'll offer
my wet fist as her reprieve

spotlit in the museum center
two violet shadows pull you in
detangling threads of childhood trauma
bruised in places, but still liplocked
still waltzing on

Love Poem, Justin Demeter

New Constellation
Justin Demeter

you're shaking the moon again, so hard
you're bruised by the stars, a fresh indigo tramp
stamp of the milky way mocking your eager
hip mottled with the whip-stain of Orion's belt
disguised as a woman dressed as a raven
singing Chappell Roan's "Casual"
you've been tenderized enough, young man, just be now
the wild hairy cut dangling from the dark
mouth of the sky
let love land on you where she wants
braille of infant moss tending the golden
warm of new bark
tangled copper limbs rafting toward a new
continent built on flowers

3I/Atlas
Jennifer Barone

at first, a deep seed
a thought of love
the hunger for it
catapults you toward Mars
in a blast of light

what potential you've initiated
pings against a million suns
the trajectory of your desire

moves toward Venus
in her underworld
absorbing roses
blossoming in sweetness

I wait
a fertile planet
orbit in spirals of love
snake into myself

don't sleep
under the new moon
we are in the darkest night
inside the heart
a black hole
devours the universe
without end

your loneliness
is just the catalyst
emptiness contains
enough vastness
to awaken us

Abrazo, Adrian Arias

Even Though You're Not Here
Jennifer Barone

the bookstore owner
has your nose
your angled chin
as he tilts his head
to show me
the poetry section

the fisherman has
the curve of your bicep
pulling up his ropes
and your hands
as he begins to scale fish

the waiter has your eyes
I call him over
to ask for salt
then more lemon
just to see you again

if too much time passes
you visit me in dreams
to tell me
all the things
you are afraid to say
or hold me in your arms
without saying a word

it is here
my longing fades
when I place my cheek
against your heart
and listen to you
breathe

Illuminations
Gianmaria Franchini

Una finestra illuminata in una notte buia
During the night I read and write,
Conjure the places we've been, giving them form
To make them gifts, as they've been to me

I draw close, recalling the shapes
Sounding the heart with a thin instrument
As rain makes birds amorous
As one tries to touch moonlight

In Los Angeles, you cradle my hand
To your jaw and bite, playful as a seal.
In the high Mojave near Hesperia
Ranchers turn their backs to suck their engines—
These places run parallel to memory now

Whales breach along the coast of Big Sur
Mysterious as a stranger's dream,
Their six-ton hearts stirring for millennia.
The tourists turn in the wind—
What immeasurable aches, they imagine
Such relief in the arms of the sea

Further on the lights go out and
There's another me and another you
         stumbling through the dark, past the lake we swim in
the river inside me   or
            the one we sleep next to

You couldn't lie if you tried.
Like your grandfather—I know only his house,
the blue of his swimming pool and your mermaid Grandmother,
who dresses but never swims

The last picture is always there.
In a window framed by darkness, there is
Your body: pale, opalescent, almost blue,
bathed in light

Ciao, Stella Mattina

Anne Marie Wenzel

In the darkness of early day,
I step out and gaze through the branches of the trees at
Venus. She hangs below the waning crescent moon,
brilliant. My heart quickens. I bask in her love until
the cool morning air nudges me into the kitchen
where I grind beans and brew fresh espresso.
I carry my cup outside and sit and sip and gaze
up at her, content in the morning twilight.

The Color of Rain: The Color of Sleep
Hollie Hardy

I rearrange the rainbow to make room
but you are already here

On a sizzling summer night in Texas, the color of rain
when the power goes out and there's nothing to do
but fuck in sweaty candlelight

The sea foam color you picked out for my toes
because it reminded you of Alabama
Whirly in True Romance and because kinda trashy
can also be kinda hot

The gray-fox-at-dusk color of my hair in middle age

In the swelter and sway of live music, strangers' laughter
lust in a smoky dive bar with dirt floors and sticky tables
the moody blue air condensing around us like sadness

Things I shouldn't have said
turn yellow—not a sun but the curling
of torn pages touched by firelight

And I am in a fire-stealing mood
a transgression shaped like kindness

Which is the color
of flesh—
yours or mine?

Still the fire
smolders

There is no other version of this story
just repetitions of color

I wake up in the undreaming night
to measure our darkness like a rainbow

The color of sleep's opacity: starlight

Your soft breath on my face: a universe

Ghazal on Fire
Hollie Hardy

Warmth runs through my blood like a wildfire of want.
My fractured heliotrope heart throbbing highway of want.

I offer the green of eyes and forest and breath and burning
for your return. These days of absence, a chasm of want.

Wherefore are thee awake, Romeo? Caffeine and longing?
Unquiet machinations of a restless repining mind? I want

To lick your body like flames, pretty pieces of broken sky
To decorate my bedroom with your bones riven of want.

I shall name myself Incandescent shine in your ribcage
like a search light seeking your flesh burning with want.

Morning
Sara Biel

—An Aubade for Jason

Your absence is just beginning
to take shape.
I wake too early
with the blade of missing
cut into my dreams.

These days light moves
like water,
finds its way in
fusses the cracks
until it forces another morning.

I sit, coffee gone cold,
all my words fallen away.
The wind pulls yellow leaves
across wet sidewalk.

Your face assembles
itself in my mind,
your eyes—unsettled questions
head tilted, waiting
for me to catch up.

I know how to walk with this stone in my shoe.
I learned from you to press
on a bruise
to bring the sharp ache
the one that makes memory blaze.

I tell myself to breathe
like you are still here,
like you are somewhere
around the corner
just beyond

my line of sight.

This Ordinary Morning Demanding Impossibles
E.K. Keith

The spaceships are crumbling
falling from the sky

It's been raining all day long
and I can't help but hope for the sun

The audience is always right
light is
particle
and   or   but
wave

Who am I
to think I can define
who I am
like the light

It's the fact that returns   I'm not
the center of the universe
except when theoretically I have to be

The spaceships are crumbling
and the weather is beautiful here

The sun behind clouds

I'm trying to think of a way
to tell you how I feel without using the word love and
I failed again

So what
if all I can offer you
is disappointment

I am like the light
my behavior changes
depending on how I'm observed

How can I help it
when you look at me like that

Requiem to the Holy Mysteries
Peggy Morrison

All night I shivered, an unsung astronaut
      flung away into black

Now I mull muted purples, nightfall
      your shape in the boundary between winds
      where we crouched saltwet slate

And I awake into dreamlight brightness
      haunted by the erotic vision
      your hero's return through a
      rainbow of jungle mist

Down in the dark mulch under the trees your face
      diaphanous meticulous
      the orange salamander in your pale hand

In molten mythological darkness
      Union of dreams
      You bring to me the dark and holy
      Mysteries
      A shadowy womb

Foreplay
Jeffrey Bryant

below my lips
I spilt another line
from a new poem.
go ahead,

lick it into your throat
in the time honored
oral tradition.
savor it, then

draw it back across my tongue
as a way of confirming
I'm not entirely
out of my mind.

our whole relationship
has been one appetizer
after another. hey!
are you going to finish that,

that which you gingerly bit
between my spread
expectations?
pour me another Pinot.

overture me

into ecstasy,
raise the curtain,
turn off your phone,

and listen to my touch.
what's to become of us?
the answer is underripe.
the answer awaits the harvest.

The Snack Bar at the Met
Jeffrey Bryant

don't pull me from this skin yet.
I'm falling in love, damn it,
and it's far from ideal.
turn off the news
and just leave me
inside an oratorio
to an illustrated man
where he's the tenor
and I'm the aria in his throat.
Milk Duds
are sold at the Met snack bar!
I just want to live long enough
to set one on his tongue
in our box
just before Mimi dies
in *La Bohème,*
to swirl in his mouth and
slowly turn his tears
into milk chocolate.
we all have our reasons to live.
this is mine,
one last chance
before I go
to take someone's breath away.

I Need You Like Hydrogen Needs A Match
Bear

So strike it
and watch me nosedive
in a ball of zeppelin fire

a smoldering skeletal husk
of papery ash, melted metal
and thick smoke.

I know where the exits are,
I watched the safety videos,
I am prepared

for the Hindenburg disaster
I will be torched into. So come on baby
light my fire!

Breach

Val DeBarra

my heart is still
a building after the fire
windows blown,
ash in the sinks.
i am not meant
to host anyone yet.

then you arrive
with your careful hands, your
voice like a locked drawer,
everything in its place.

this shouldn't happen.

the timing is wrong
in a way that has teeth.
the ethics hum
like live wire in the
walls. whatever this is,
it knows its own consequences.

i am unfinished.
you are positioned.
the space between us
is supervised.

and still

something slips its leash not touch
not confession
a pressure shift

a quiet click
like a door sealing
from the inside.

by the time we name it
the body has signed.

Marcus
Natasha Dennerstein

Your partner has another partner and you see her presence everywhere:
the knot in the bread bag surely tied by Rosalia.

Your perfume bottle has its cap removed, which you always put
back on: evidence of the presence of Rosalia.

You demand of Marcus not to have her in your house, but every
time you go to work you return to see signs and symptoms of Rosalia.

You see her markings everywhere and don't know if its gaslighting,
your imagination or a game played by Rosalia.

You cook him a complicated meal but when he returns he has no
appetite as most likely he already ate with the curséd Rosalia.

The TV stations are set to *Natasha's favorites* but viewer choices
have been changed forever by that goddam Rosalia.

Green Space
Egan Reeve

on the day I was to meet him

        made sure my trousers had deep pockets

squeezed my sad into a zip-lock bag

        sealed it nice and tight

three weeks post-farewell

        our sanctuary already had been gutted,

structure now   rooflessruthless sinking soggy

        throwing shapes across my face

    skeleton of times before   locale of shelter   hiding

a time to take pause and sit with   **LOVE**   (its loss)

    he smokes a rollie   already in his pocket

but the lack of shade is

        threatening

    I worry the fire from his fingers can't   or

    won't well take the breeze

already in his hands soft as spinach leaves fresh picked, sturdy
asparagus-esque arteries, hearty stew brewing in the body of
the beast, he sips and draws the nicotine through early summer
dry chapped lips, the fag goes out, but we are exposed already,
in this apparent construction site, raised beds just out of reach,
when he gently says lets go back home – the feeling in my gut the
steady unwell slithering, the reptiles without feet, and if we were
different men, built by god and
not   self made as martyrs of contention -

the
        bag

        inside   my   pocket

        leaks.

Paloma
Luisa Guilianetti

Thank you for choosing us—again.
Choosing again to nest in our hanging basket.
Bed of loose twigs below the rose geranium.

Last month, I watched your long-tailed mate
coo insistently, loop the morning sky
court you with his aerial acrobatics.

Thank you for inviting me to slow down.
                Pause
at the hallway window   witness

how you alternate feeding and incubating
duties, keeping your young warm
beneath your speckled brown bodies.

When you leave them alone, I worry.
Thank you for reminding me that we must
prepare our young to fend for themselves.

Soon the two chicks nestle below
our porch bench. Inch into the light. You watch
from the telephone line. Return at night.

Afternoon flying lessons along the back fence.
Small skips across the top beam, nosedives
to the ground below the olallieberry vines.

You teach them to forage, to recognize threats.
One chick flew from the fence top to the yellow
chair beside me.   Stayed a while.

Thank you for flight in this unraveling
war-drunk world. Sweet song amidst
grating speeches and belting lies.

My birder friend says you return because
you feel safe. I walk to the window past my kids'
empty rooms. What we create to hold us.

Demeter
Luisa Guilianetti

Day and night, I search for you. Roam field, forest
and shore until I drop like a cracked skull.
Even poppies belie relief. My tears stone the earth.
My fury starves it: vines wither, no seed sprouts.

I see your fingers first—pomegranate-stained—clawing
from a slit of scarred ground. You inch yourself up. Flaxen
hair tangled by sex and grave dust. Hips newly curved.
Your eyes wary of light.   Or have you forgotten my face?

The earth wakens where you step. Sorrel, purslane
and clover carpet your path back to me. Dewy leaves
unfurl on naked boughs. The air warms, pours light
into stone jars.   Then it is spring.

Untitled, Kyle Knobel

Everything I Know About Love Fits Into This Monopoly Thimble
DJ Benhaim

You'd think love
would need more space—
a room, a bed,
the wide acreage of belief—
but mine lives here,
a tin cradle
for a plastic hand.

It's small, I know—
barely room
for a swallowed apology,
for a die held in the mouth—
the sharp click of a door
never taught
to close softly.

Inside, there's just enough air
for a single memory:
your honeyed voice grazing
my ear
like a fingertip testing a stream;
your laughter, light as lint,
as if the world
were thin enough to float.

Sometimes I tip it over
to hear the sound—
that hollow knock—
and imagine
every hand I trusted
testing the seams,
straining to grow.

But love,
the kind I know best,
stays small:
a keepsake,
a pocket-sized shelter
for the part of me
still learning
how *not* to split
when someone
reaches for it.

Hold it to the light and you'll see
the history of touch shrunk to a pinprick:

Mama threading a needle
through a torn sleeve;
Pops palming change
as if each coin
were a promise
to be kept;
the way I once held
a sweetheart's name
until it dissolved,
in salt and rain.

So yes,
all that I know of love
fits neatly into
this thimble—

honoring
the rules
I was given.

El Beso, by Adrian Arias

Love Snores
Adrian Arias

Love snores
and wakes entire towns.
It doesn't know how to use dictionaries,
delights in crooked tongue twisters
and baroque insults.

And how do I know these things about love?

Because one day it knocked on my door.
I opened.
I was afraid,
I wanted to run,
but I faced it.
I was drawn to its rough face
and its bulging eyes,
as if they couldn't fit inside the world.

It was hungry for me.
So I undressed slowly
and opened my arms.
I let it devour me,
bite by bite.

And in the middle of the night I woke up,
because it was snoring with such happiness
that I stayed by its side,
adoring it.

New Birds
M.G. Martin

new birds will be invented
to carry the noise of us

new birds in flight
singing our libretto
some new thing
older than love

new birds with wings
named after lakes

for the new birds
we vibrate the air
our sound is massive

hear not new birds
when the wind feels
sad & pixilated
look to the horizon
& listen
use your new bird ears
to hear us putting leaves
on the trees
fear us playing spring

new birds we wish you
luck in the infinite sky
where maps make
no sense
where our echo
will never betray
its name
it's us

o new birds
take our song
into the third
year of us
take it beyond
the speed of sound
to what can be
imagined but not
heard

new birds in our sheets
and hair and the place
we did not know
to exist
until we did

until our skin
becomes birds
and the skies
fill with us

My Dragon
M.G. Martin

a common dragon can thrive
on only flowers that
pollinate by moonlight

you are not common
your energy is medieval   uncanny

it is your duty
to extort the village
on account of your diamond blood
it doesn't matter
if you can't help
                it
you are from the sea of scales
aquatic leather
& feather

your vibe is wide

you are green fire
the flame from
the sky

Hopelandic
Len Kuntz

     I want to speak Hopelandic with you because nothing else matters. I want to spill gibberish across your skin in silly dapples, sift through the clouds of your hair, climb your chin, toss copper pennies from your toes, write a sonnet with the haughty tautness of your left nipple. And you can brush all of your rubbish against my spine or hippocampus, take a mint vacation, let your fingers chatter and decode atoms in the ether. If you twitch, I'll catch your vowels, suck on your consonants, bathe in your conjunctions. I'll paint you meringue, make you flowers from the sheer wing of disorder. Together we'll gather the night, unstitch every dream, tie them around our tongues and swallow when we're good and ready.

Mount of Venus
James J. Siegel

I want to believe
all the cups in this Celtic Cross you dealt
are really meant for me. An abundance
of chalices, the Star in my crown
and Empress in my house.

I've been let down
by spellcasting, black candles we use
to burn shadows into walls,
and in those shadows we search
for things we never find,
wings of messenger angels,
Gabriel at the Annunciation.

When I was young
I could put full faith in these fantasies,
sun and moon standing still, newspaper
horoscopes with lucky numbers. Suddenly,
sixes and nines wherever I go,
on house doors and telephone extensions,
perfect psychic geometry.

But in my age
I stopped believing everything adds up,
aligns—the time I was born,
the position of the stars reading me
like a mood ring, my Capricorn cusp
tossing me about the earth and air.

I want to believe
the Chinese Zodiac. My Horse
compatible with your Dog, but
I've always summoned Snakes
and Goats into the orbit of my ether.
How nice to have a year to call your own,
12 months of prosperity, luck and love.

But I don't believe—
not until my hand slides into yours
and I feel the delicate drag of your finger
along the crevices of my heart and head,
your soft drift over my Jupiter and Saturn
to point out the pattern of my future,
the warm vibration of you
circling,
        circling
the terrain of Venus.

My Mother Says
James J. Siegel

        My mother says,
You've never written a poem about me.
I hear the disappointment in her voice.
        It's true,
           I've written poems about my father
           even my grandmother,
and I can tell she blames herself
because I am nothing
if not my mother's son
and I too would blame myself
if I could not find myself
in the stanzas of someone I love.

        But I've never told my mother
how many times I've tried
to conjure her in couplets
and failed to unspool lines
fine enough to immortalize her.
I only find the shape of my shadow
falling on the tundra of a blank page,
and if I traced the silhouette of my face
I would sketch out my mother's cheekbones,
the deep, long reach of her lashes.

Even the way I hold a pencil—
a left-handed grip in my right hand—
a habit I picked up from my mother,
the reason why my journals are litanies
of chicken scratch.
        Line after line of crooked letters
I struggled to string together poems
and only let loose a deep-bodily sigh,
an exasperation I heard a million times

from my mother when I was a child
and forgot a sink full of dirty dishes,
an unmade bed.
But sometimes I'm able to pull a thread
that leads to the center of something gold,
poems where I've found my home—
        the Ohio of my youth I left behind
to build a life in San Francisco,
to build poems like little houses
clinging to the hills and clouds.

Those are the poems I hold tight to
because they feel the Pacific in their hair
and sleep peaceful under the night fog
because my mother once said,
    Don't live your life regretting
the things you didn't do.

And that too is a poem—
one my mother wrote before I was born,
a sonnet of sorrow
for the lives she never lived,
for choosing the life others chose for her.

So when I told her my life was calling
from shores thousands of miles away
my mother cried,
    and held me,
        and let me go
to write my own poems.

In my strange calligraphy,
in every love letter I've written to my life,
she has been there all along,
writing along with me, living
in each line and word
I've breathed into being.

Dreamcatcher
K.R. Morrison

I remember that day. There's a ghost
trapped in weathered photograph, conjured

>from severed   hearts   supervised
>visits   insulting   their surveillance.

>She hugged me goodbye
>like our lives depended on it.

>Arms of amethyst
>she tried to keep my loss of her   away

>but I always found remnants.   Her golden hair
>mother in my pockets   mother heart

>staring heavy back at me from amber barbells   above

>cheekbones carved into arrowheads.   Outlaw
>mothers stew in firebird grief they feed

>with men's blood & gasoline.   Staring at her
>sepia face   I can still smell her

>in her gaze there is a torch
>that 40 years later   summons me

>our visits.   Her Motown records
>Diana Ross & The Supremes   her paintbrush

>singing. My mother had a way of creating
>countries from her sadness

>>our love a nation
>>under dreamcatcher.

Motherland
Char Lacsina

I left when I was three,
small enough to be carried,
old enough that my bones still remember
the weight of being held.

Coming back feels like stepping into a room
mid-conversation.
The walls are talking.
The air smells like heat and fried garlic and rain
that never quite leaves.
I know this place.
I don't know this place.
Both truths rest in my chest
without asking to be resolved.

At Sunset, people gather outside churches
with candles thinning in their hands.
Outside the gates, steam rises—
puto bumbong wrapped in banana leaves,
hands blackened with charcoal,
sugar and butter softening purple rice.
Faith stands beside hunger.
No one explains it.
They eat.

My aunt says, *Welcome home.*
Her voice is steady, ordinary,
as if home has always been here.
Something in me loosens.
Something keeps watch.

In my grandparents' house,
time leans against the furniture.
Their absence hums—
not loud,
not cruel,
just present.
I know where my grandmother should be standing.
I know the sound my grandfather would make
before speaking.
The knowing hurts.
The knowing holds.
I move room to room,
touching corners, doorframes, dust.
This house has known love
without witnesses.
I feel like a visitor
who somehow belongs.
Palabok stains my fingers orange.
Sweet, salty, alive.
I eat slowly,
as if staying is something the body remembers
before the mind does.

On the jeepney, metal rattles.
Voices overlap—
bayad po—
passed hand to hand.
The road carries us.
My body sways.
It knows this.

Before I leave Pampanga,
I bring flowers.
Light in my hands.
Heavy in my throat.
I place them down.
I don't say much.
Some things are understood
by being done.

This land does not ask me to choose.
It lets me be layered—
leaving and returning,
grief and gratitude,
a child who left
and a woman learning how to arrive.

I want more mornings.
More listening.
I want to meet this place again and again
until it stops feeling like memory
and starts feeling like breath.

Malagu

Florida Clay
Victoria Dym

Torn by metal claw, the baked Florida soil is turned,
        excavated, drilled, tested—
homeless nightcrawlers dig deep into the day's uprooted mounds.

We lay our blanket down.

After Mexican dinner, we forego the movie, take a drive instead—
        heat from the
setting sun in our faces, heat from the food in our bellies.

We lay our blanket down.

New 250K and up—under construction, the printed sign,
        Hidden Lakes—dwellings
in various stages of completion, plotted around a lake—
        It's Lakeland, after all.

We lay our blanket down.

There is space and emptiness. Silence too—no dogs behind
        front doors who bark as we pass by. Silence
in the stars and between us. Big Dipper—Little Dipper.

We lay our blanket down.

Like a flag for our new-found love, we lay our blanket down—
        an outdoor bed, this
outdoor room, this Florida clay—forgive us our trespasses.

A Love Song for the City Before I Go
Joseph Voth

          New York, I loved
The thought of you, loved your pickpocket sermon at midnight
When nothing more than the moon's half-reflected face in a
Puddle gathering on Christopher Street—and the worn shoes

Stirring the puddle as they stepped casually into it,
The oil dropped there by delivery trucks, all blues and chalk-

Whites in darkness, rippling at the face in water—was love,
A fact for which I can't apologize, Your Honor,
             Conscience, ghost,

And wouldn't if I could.

      I have turned enough stones for a lifetime.

Let the pulled pork and collard greens of Harlem be love,

And the waitress in her taupe and weary shoes as the hours
Before dawn tumble through her—love hiding in the seams

Of daylight;

      And the counterfeit watches gnashing in a
Briefcase as their seller jumps the turnstile at Fulton Street

And slides into the 4-line and the cop who gives chase,
Loses him at the turnstile;

           And the hard-stump tongues
Of Astoria, loosened toward the dream inside a cup,

Love; and Coltrane under garden lights on Fourth Street, a Love
Supreme;

   And every face under a bar light and both my fists
Numb with grief or clenched in anger and my head bowed in the

Disbelief reserved for fools when I say, "I loved you, New York,"

And you, in your luminous body, closing the door still warped
From winter behind you.
    ~

     It's time I put myself to bed.
The light at the kitchen table has shuffled off and I'm tired.

I will waken far from you, in the high country near a lake.
I should say a prayer before sleep. I should mention your name.

No use wringing your hands. It was all for the best, you see?
It was all for the nothing that was and the nothing that is.

It's time I put this all to sleep.

A Brief History of How the Heart Breaks
Joseph Voth

—for Ron Champagne

Everywhere,
Morning steps where it can,

As a houseguest might,
Lifting one foot

From the groaning floorboard
Before the other drops

And the sleeping host stirs.
The house returns

To its silence, the daybreak
To its quiet. You've known this

Or you haven't, this breath
Held at the doorway

Of an empty house, the rain
Outside, calling. You've

Listened too, or have you
Slept right through it

Dreaming, as the living do,
Of the heart that waits

Patiently in heavenly grass?

For My Husband Sleeping on the Floor Near Our Dying Dog
Michelle Patton

Second marriage, no child
together—this rescue, this corgi mix
who thinks herself a noble shepherd
became our only child.

If I could paint or make a movie
or birth a pair of wings and become
an archeologist of air, maybe
you could see him:
in his blue velour bathrobe on the floor
snoring a perfect cartoon snore.

Would you understand then?
This man who tells me now and then
where we'll live when we're rich: half the year in Spain
half in Manhattan. Every time
a new paradise he measures out. We'll never
remember all the places we've been,

the dirty towns and small cafes,
but when I tell you I have hitched my wagon
to this man, and this smelly dog,
I mean I want to lay my body down
and be their shelter, be their lucky earth.

Between Two Raging Bulls
Michelle Patton

Sacred Sunday means we do no work,
we do no chores. Today I made
biscuits and gravy and you said
Hey, wanna watch Raging Bull?
Sure, I said. You say *I can't believe*
you've never watched this before!
I said we've had this conversation.

New York, we were first dating
and we had a small scuffle, an early fight.
You were walking ahead of me on the avenue
and you turned and said *Baby*
let's be friends! Then laughed
and said it again. I was so in love
and taken with that phrase.

Today, I let myself go, let myself
love what you love, and my god
if I was not lifted right out of my own
small life. The arc of De Niro and Pesci,
I mean. I make you fast forward

through the worst of the rage,
and you do though it kills
you just a little. My dear nerd
you're right, and furthermore
thank you. Maybe one day

if there is still an America
we will take another road trip—
Peach Snapple and peanuts for you,
nicotine and cannabis for me.
and you'll say *remember how*

you had never seen Raging Bull?

Tanta Paz: So Much Peace
Alexandria Giardino

    We have seen so much by now
    taken measure of our identical elongated hands
    accumulated words for one another to understand
    traversed war-torn landscapes, brutal and magical
    unfurled our palms along narrow Pacific highways
    stormed each other's limits and come back finally
    from gazing at a bravely dreamt canal
    to the torment in this volcanic valley
    full of market life, commerce for our fantasies
    generous Mexico, gives up space for us
    to live every moment as if we were awake
    with our eyes closed in her labyrinthine excesses.

Tanta paz siempre llega tarde.

      So much peace always comes too late.

Snow
Patrick Cahill

He ordered a vodka, a breeze to sweeten the dark street, music that burned whatever skin it happened to touch, clouds that drifted beyond their understanding of water, as flocks rose through flakes of falling snow and into the depths of the sky, the vodka half gone as an image of her stepping from the shower flickered, a drop of water suspended from one earlobe, then went out—a flute's intimation of rising birds, an oboe's of snow flecks on a wolf's snout.

The Peach Fuzz on Your Knuckles
Lourdes Figueroa

pond the great *pond* of your eyes
fireflies skipping on the water of your iris
I meant skimming—a task so wondrous
as their legs prickle the still
water—the deep dark of your iris
was the cenote I couldn't bear to swim in
a bellicose voz or maybe it was melancholy like sweet bubble
gum when you first pop it in your mouth
in this way I learned
lost gestures in between my body &
yours in this way poetry finally arrived
me chasing you as you pulled the night over your head the
peach fuzz on your knuckles
the quiet time in your car the air conditioning buzzing cool &
my soul stood outside the car watching us both
that day the rarest comet in our lifetime skimmed the skyline as
it began to lavender itself to bed
                        but this is how some of it really happened
from the inside
came the sound of crickets
the sweetness of carnation flower
the grass smell
purring chest bones
our gibbous eyes & the pond outside reflecting
the departure of day
the quiet arrival of time
& your fingers touched the side of my hip.

Come Home

Lourdes Figueroa

Non-consensual:

prayers

children of night born

a plastic fairy tale

night after night
I drive
& think of her

she smiles so bright

am I locked up in a smile?

what is the sun's reach?

what is she reaching towards when we sleep?

the skin of my elbow
I pinched it while we were staring out to sea

the night wind biting our cheeks

& the distinct word opulence sounded good in my brain

thinking about the arrival of aliens

would they like to join us
for breakfast?

at night while driving you home
I kept these Lorca lines warm in my armpit

> *Loneliness w/o rest!*
> *The little eyes of my body*
> *& the big eyes of my horse*
> *never close at night*

///
I arrived with soft fur pressed against my cheek
rasgitos de luna entera de anoche todavia encima de mi panza
a belly rising and falling
my hands under my knees
my body sits on the only chair in the room
it was here before all us
what I remember the most is the silver bracelet around a wrist
the pieces of gravel imbedded in the torso of my palm
your small hand on my shin
what I remember the most es un pasillo oscuro con niña pequeña
acurrucando
nene pequeño
the last person to save my life was the woman from last night's gathering
of bodies & voices of sweaters, possible sentences, clipped verbs,

she said acabo de salir un infierno sali de la carcel de ice
the last person to save my life was my brother
                                            come home come home

here the portal is the sky meeting us
at the exact spot where there is a division b/w earth
& where I am becoming a small glimpse of time
the light between two yellow leaves of ginkgo tree
        on the coldest winter morning

Orchard of the Body
Brittiany Lema

Your shoulder tasted faintly of salt,
sun,
and the long day you carried
before you came to me.
I pressed my face there,
breathing you in,
learning the climate of your
warmth. We fit without effort
hips aligning like instinct,
like something ancient recognizing itself.
Outside, crickets stitched the dark together.
Inside, the slow ripening
touch to touch,
heat building not to break
but to deepen.
Love, I've learned,
is not always urgency.
Sometimes it is harvest
the patient sweetness
of what has been tended
with care.
I carried you with me afterward,
under my ribs,
where hunger and gratitude
share the same language.

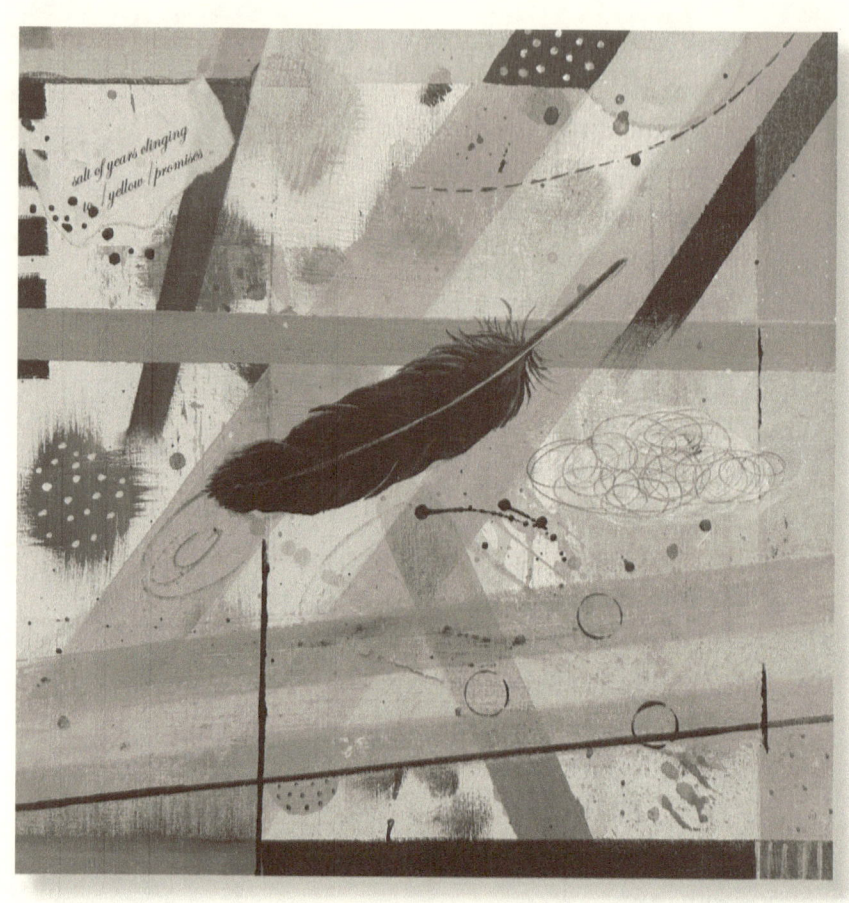

Salt of Years, by Candace Loheed

Sweet Fruit
Candace Loheed

alone
lying on my bed,
the light low
I'd been reading for
while when
I put down my book
and began to think
about you
with sweet fruit
resting in your palm.
I could see you so clearly
your hands
even though
you are so far away
and it seems so long.
you cut straight
to the core,
ripe, saffron colored fruit
splayed
by your touch.
your knife,
your wrist,
accomplice in this motion.
my mouth
watered
and
I envied the fruit
of my imaginings,
heading for
your mouth.

Bed 'n Breakfast
Al Averbach

Day sifts into the dark,
loosens night's fist,
fritters at eyelashes.

      Sleep uncurls.

Already she's out of bed.
Appetite on dawn patrol,
stomach stalking.

      A sweet breeze mosies by

scent off the simmering onion
and the sun slowly rises in his head
on vapors of the dark caffeine.

      With these grits I thee wed.

Light coming up the coverlet.
Dream back in for a last swim.
Morning butter's up

      melting in the land.

Earthbound (don't come after me)
Shizue Seigel

Why would I want to dig up the dead—
rocking rides in the big blue Chrysler—
whispering dreams into each other's necks
                      discreetly curtained
                      by Marina Green mist.

Don't tempt me to shovel up
        cracked mirrors and broken promises from the landfill.
The carnies took their coke and left town decades ago—
Bottlenecks the color of stormy seas
        stretched shrill by ambitious heat that existed only for itself
A hall of mirrors warming no one.
        Do you miss the vision reflected in my eyes?

What is the sound of an unstrung guitar.
        a broken pick
           thrill rides rusting in the sand?
Oh, your hips, your eyes, your teeth!
        Why dig up the heat that smolders without warmth?
        Buckskin fringe and sequins scattered like fish scales in the dirt.

Decades after you became a ghost to me
you show up evergreen
        restored to the Michigan woods
digitally resurrected and
        haunting my posts to make amends.
I won't reach out. I'd rather
        leave my last memory "address unknown"
                desiccating in some Nevada desert
                dreaming with the lizards
                and tumbling, tumbling over yourself.

Blow on in the wind.
        Don't come after me!
            I'll take life straight.

There Are More Beautiful Things Than Aditya Roy Kapur
Elizabeth Shanaz

—*after Morgan Parker*

The rent left your account when Aditya posted
his abdomen bathed in the sunrise.
You counted his muscles, imagined them pressed on your skin.
A man has never felt safe to you, not completely anyway.
A glass fell in the sink and you remembered
the way your heart ripped itself into shards of weaponry
that you wished would slit you right open, to sky, to sea.
That was when he stared moodily onto your feed
holding your gaze and a dozen sponsored tags.
You clean the sink and let him take you on the counter,
the spice rack collapsing in your dance, you think.
Or maybe by the bookcase, with trade paperbacks raining
down like rice grains after the *pheras*.
You type his handle into the search bar and waltz your finger
through a gridwork of endless promotion.
Breathless at the idea of being close enough to count his arm hairs or
beads of calisthenics sweat,
of spiritually tenanting a heroine's legs and wrapping them around his neck.
You gorgeous girl, there are more beautiful things than Aditya Roy Kapur:
You, for one.
Your dada blowing *du'as* on your scalp.
Kati rolls with extra meat, you can only rip into them with your molars.

A Carrara marble floor covered in the fragmented debris
    of a pattern you never thought you'd break.
A poem so buried in metaphor you can never quite get it.
The kaleidoscope sand of tea fastened to a cup's bottom
    filled with fortunes to deliver.
Champagne embroidery on a tissue *dupatta*.
Fingernail dirt that comes out in one unbroken piece.
The moment you start to pee after holding it just a little too long.
Digging your nose after being in public all day.
A child's smile of uneven teeth, children don't just trust anyone.
Telling a joke that fucking lands.
Peeling the plastic off of something brand new.
Hitting "skip ad" before the button disappears.
A sneeze that finally comes after playing hard to get.
Getting to overhear your neighbor's juicy argument.
A driver giving you a pass on a highway hustling with blur.

I swear one day you will wake up and not even check his page,
your eyes too busy undoing the beauty of your pinky toe alone.
Too busy wondering when you stopped crying at the smell of rainfall,
when you started tasting so good.

lovvve
Tom Batchelder

sent to

unearthed by

me

visibly invisible

i claim certainty

delusion fueling

warned by all

blinded by my ascension

tumbling towards the sun

Tender Hearts Club
Ingrid Keir

The first hour we met
you asked me to marry you

my red lips all over you
kissing in public

uncommon display
maybe the universe

wants to show me love exists
without expectation or stronghold

your mouthed last words
you are magic

Mezcal smoke on your breath

Come with me
your eyes pleaded

Aries full moon
potent waxing and waning

I want to be the drink
on your tongue

instead
I write you poems

I'll never send

Afterglow
Ingrid Keir

    The wind blows and I feel my nipples rise
                    Arousal
        in every leaf
               language of rustle
                        allure of moonsong
                bow of kundalini
                        snakes playing in curvature

Consider the body's frame
        shoulder slides into back
collarbone rests above a naked chest
        lungs expand
        the softness of longing

I hunger to taste your mouth
                words fail
passion   like the wind
suddenly and out of nowhere
        taken up like a kite
           in flight   glide dips and dances

I feel your glow
                moving closer
eyes commemorate my body
a starry phosphorescence

I want you to play me like the harp
make me sing while we recreate
the music of spheres

I watch the moonrise
        across the horizon
night sky laced with a golden orb

the tattoo on your forearm comes to mind
I trace it with my fingers
        a circle
        no beginning
        no end
after
        afterglow
my fingertip pulsed with electricity
        the portal

O rush of perfume and possibility
of rose petals and wind

Things That Make You Remember Dreams
Kary Hess

A field of grass
When he said "there's something on your shoulder"
The sky's stillness
Wallpaper patterns
Scraps of paper on the table
A random occurrence at the post office
That kid letting go of their balloon on purpose
Lichen patterns on the back fence
When she laughed a certain way
The movement of his hands on the piano

Matrimony
Jonathan Siegel

You Make Me Want To Throw Out My Mattress
My Bed Frame
The Sheets The Blankets The Pillows & Pillowcases
Everything...
And Build On Freshly Sanctified Ground
A Place Of Indescribable Beauty
A Cove Of All That Is Delicate & Arousing To TOUCH
Unseen-Uncontaminated By Any Other's Eyes
A Cradle Of Exquisite Purity
A Divine Nook
A Shrine Of Shining Invite
An Immaculate Pristine Altar...

For Us To Do...UNHOLY Things On!

Sacrilegious Abominations
Of The Most Profane & Perverse Kind
Ever Committed Or Imagined
I Want The GODS To Watch
As I Do Things To Your Body
They Never Thought Or Dreamt Could Be Done
To Human Flesh
A Desecration Of Universal Proportions
I Want To MANGLE You

Into Positions
To Make Aphrodite, Herself Blush & Cum With Envy
I Want Zeus To Learn How It "IS"
To Truly Please A Mortal, By Our Example
And Then Watch Him As He Quickly Tries To Imitate
Only To Fail, MISERABLY

Cause What We're Gonna Do
What I'm Going To Do "TO YOU"
Takes Practice
And I've Spent My Entire Life Preparing For YOU
Learning Ev-ery Single Sexual Morsel Of Knowledge
    One Can Acquire In Hopeful Await Of YOU
Purposefully
Holding Myself Back, In Past
From Such Thorough Release
Of My Carnal Depravity
So That I May EXPLORE YOU
In Ways I Have Yet To Even Breach Before

I Want Our "First Time" To Never END
Our Initial Session Of Joining Our Parts
To Defy The Laws Of Biology
HELL
I Want Our Embrace To Bridge The Gap
Between "The Theory Of (Sensual)ativity & Quantum Ph(uck)ics"

I Want Society To Shun Us
Excommunicate Us
To Be Appalled
By Such Filthy Nasty Ceaseless Lust
That They Have No Choice But To Banish Us
To A Land Of Our Own

An EDEN
Comprised Of Sensational Expanses
Of Tropics, Savannas, Everglades & Forestry
Of INTENSE VIBRANCE
A Palate Of Such Breath-Stealing Immensity That As We Frolic
Garmentless
Conjoined Rolling In Rapturous Delight
The Varied Pigments Of Every Region
Will Stain Our Dermal Canvases
We Will Become ALL THE COLORS OF THE WORLD
Weaved Into Each Other With Passionate Brush

I Want To MAKE LOVE TO YOU
In Every Shade & Combination Of Red, Yellow, & Blue
And Paint Our Children Into Existence
Children
FREE
Of The Judgment Of One's Tone Of Skin
For Every Glorious Hue
Will Be FAMILY

I Want Our Kids
Our Land
Our Home
Our Love
Our Passion
Our Friendship
That Unpronounceable Connection We Share
Our ART Of Living LIFE
To Be The Blueprints From Which
All Other Planets Will Draw Likeness From
Attempt To Recreate
Try To Emulate
As Best As Can
But Never—Quite—Capture It...To Its Fullest

For Only You & I
Can Create Such Global Extending "Perfection Of Union"
For Our Hearts Alone AS ONE
Is Capable
Of Springing Forth Such
Brilliant Peace
But HEY

What Better Way
To Renew Our "Devotional Selves" To Each Other Than By
Traveling To Every Distant Star And Having The Obligation
Of Starting "Our Whole Affair"
Over
& OVER
Again.

Untitled
Lam Khong

With just a part of you
I see a vision
your hand or elbow
if one part of you
is all I'm allowed to see
I can still recognize you
I forget myself sometimes
discovering something new
I have not noticed before
is it possible you change
every time I see you?
You smiled when I pointed out
the dimple on your lower lip
I have not realized
how your mouth curves
almost violently at the corners
The freckles on your shoulders
just a shade darker than your skin
Your neck, more tender
And the faded red shirt
you wore this morning
which I'm certain is
the most beautiful color
I have ever seen

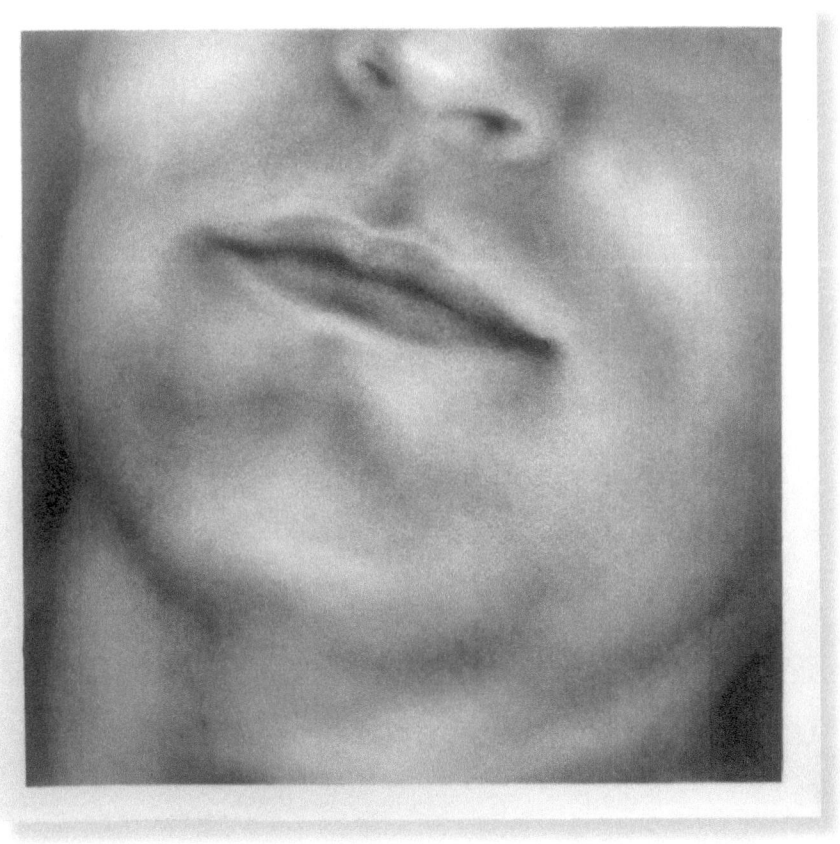

Saint John in Ecstasy, by Lam Khong

Oh My Love
Maggie La Rochelle

Oh my love you say
Frank Sinatra
you say
I want to be dancing
with you
touching you
in a kitchen.
I say
I want to wade
into the surf
with you
stars lit like bulbs
kelp swaying.
I want
to place moist leaves
of yellow and
gold on
your shoulders
and kiss them
to affix them.
I say
you are the shadow
of a strong oak
me the black walnut
in the night
you the salt
for my tongue
our feet flecking mud as we run
I want
the streams
down the hillside
window pane
smell of herbs

heat of kitchen
shone by the lone light up valley.
Oh my love you say
I say
the sun is rising over the autumn hills
       in our stomachs.

What Is Love?
Lynn Light

—after Deee-Lite

You know the song—
How do you say…

Seriously? I dunno.

A tricky thing…that love,
Trying to fool me.
Soooo mischievous.

Why would love be like this?
Clearly, love plays games.
On again,
Off again,
Hot,
Cold,
Swooning,
Deflating,
Sounds like a lame-ass roller coaster to me.
Or menopause.

REAL love wouldn't do that…right?

Whoop…there it IS.
grabbing my ass
giving me fever
a case of the ICK
and then tossing me in a compost bin.
wut?

That IS not love…is it?

Or maybe it is—
the messy, sassy kind
with bedhead and big feelings,
the kind that hides my keys
and then helps me find them.
So I'm like:
Girl, what even ARE you?

And she laughs—
That big cosmic joking laugh
the one that spins that great big disco ball in the sky
projecting a zillion splintered reflections
of me
Seemingly separate…yet projecting from the whole.
Lighting it all up…

And suddenly
I get it.

LOVE never went anywhere
Love never lied
Love never ghosted me

LOVE IS

Was
Has always been
Always will be
Here…Now
consistently…trustably…inevitably
without reservation

LOVING IT ALL.

Delectible.
Divine.

Six Pack
Elisabeth Nails

I got a man
a six pack man
and I'm talking coronas
but not beer
he winds up long strands
      of paper
And pushes them through
the platen
with a flurry of fingerstrokes
my man draws a circle
with his machines
and dances inside of it
like a flame
he spits his visions
to heal his heart
to listen deeper
to care for the world

XXXmas 2025
Phillip T. Nails

This little poem
wanted to be an extensive list
of trash items seen
in the underground subways
of New York City.

And this little poem wanted
to be the sick dog in the documentary
about a multinational team
of caretakers bonded by their feeling
the dog was a symbol
for peace in the middle east.

But some red switches got flipped
and some green levers got pulled
and some broken hearts
became dancers
that ran away to Las Vegas
to resurrect Elvis and Prince
so they could duet together
as an army of thousands of their backup singers
Parachuted over the nation's capitol
and we all knew
the revolution
was finally here.

This little poem was love
masquerading as an angel
in your panty drawer
trying to set you free.

This poem knew time was
dressed as a large chef
with a sharp knife
and waxed mustache.

This poem knew he was
standing over you
ready to casually murder your loin
in the name of flavor.

You are the present, the gift
in my soul
there is no room
for another fast fashion sweater
in my go-go bag.

Flashlight batteries shake a rhythm
as we dance in the darkness
of a heist and the diamonds are your eyes
the rubies are your nipples.

Anticipation is nakedness
nudity is churning.

Open your doors and windows
open your mind
open to what is emerging
speak to her directly.

We are a sunshine
exploding seeds across gardens
making flowers and fruit.

We are the skin
we are the vines
when we say, love
pass it on.

We are the dirt and
every star
in the sky
we are the vibrations
I'm sure you've heard.

We are the music
made with dusty instruments
riding analog tape ribbon
into history
we are hidden black walnut ink
we are glitter
we are silvery tattoos on goths.

We are not overpriced drinks
get that shit away from me.

Cue the saxophone
I am a siren's song
in the afterglow of a hot flash
kiss me in the dawn
i am dangling cool desire
on frayed string
preaching to the choir
this mess is our mess.

There is no problem on our planet
that does not belong
to all of us
that is the love I want to
talk with you about
at the edge of the sweetest spanking.

I am on sale
I am actual cost
I am real
love is real
love is in the rain
water is life
the land is holy
you are the water running
through the land
nothing is more real
than the wet poem that is you
moving time like a patient mountain
across the earth
as the sea rises and falls.

We Shall Call It Love
Brian Cronwell

1.
What a pleasure to meet
in the spacious intimacy
of strangers,
before shame is invented.

—Chana Bloch

in the hottub sky's
shuffle, we are
asterisks and
white blips of
mosquitoes in
citronellasmoke.
clouds and
jetspray lightflash,
and you talk,
soft words of
lowtide waves in
dark motion. stay
in this gentleeasy
distance, how
nightsky drifts,
oh, more floattalk.
the wind brushes
by water and
airspray, silence's
quietbubbling yes
and thanks for smile's
sweat, rising, rising.

2.
If predatory flowers
have blossomed in you
let me be the lost bee.

—Edvin Sugarev

nothing surprises me   finding us naked
skidding from dream to wake
to in between   arms draped   legs braided
damp hair rolling like landshelves   on faultlines
the cling-peach-october moon's recital
trembling sheets   late-night kisses   quilt-tighter
nothing knows the name of fear now   safety
in the senses   breathing gladly   dripping rain

daring to loose gusts   trading the past
(something here disturbs me   ice-cube
losing shape   outside the freezer   awake
when i wake   well you   know   too)
tense for eternal present   (curling
against my chest   my heart beating
like a slowing drum)   secure   in the embrace
of   (never mind   we are waking now)
such ready wings

3.
Your body, salt marshes where I reign in thirst.

—Jean Senac

as the brief rain is
saliva on the desert
that in time dries
and cracks, so

the dreams i
wake from resurge.
in the sounds of this
night, i, silent as
wheat, hear the slow
subtle call of
acceptance, the unseen
hand that clasps
mine and leads me to water.

4.
And so it was I entered the broken world
to trace the visionary company of love.

        —Hart Crane

the crescent of your thumbnail shining
just before you press it between my lips,
like a lunar eclipse with my tides, yours,
oars that draw us across a bay, the way
sweat's debt to truth discerns the yearning,
culled and called sacred by some, profane
by another's fear, like rocks piled
into a scree-fort against the unknown,
perhaps ourselves, or the wonder
of an onion's inner layers just before
nothing: your skin my sacrament,
i drink your saliva, eat your moist hairs.
whatever others may call it,
we shall call it love.

Octavia
Maw Shein Win

yesterday sent an email for a friend's celebration of life

today I looked through my phone for photos:

a backyard birthday party w/ colored hats & champagne

on a swing set w/ her daughter dressed as an anime character

a group of old punks in black ratty sweaters at the roxie theater

days after another chemo treatment, looking down at her phone

sitting on a chair w/ her husband behind her

two of us, heads touching

Octavia
Maw Shein Win

we all had crooked bangs back then

when we'd cut them ourselves or our sisters would

sometimes we'd cry when we'd look in the mirror

we'd mirror each other's moves as we danced around

when we sang we'd laugh at our songs

sometimes on key but usually off

we'd forget about the crooked bangs

when we'd snap our fingers all at the same time

By The Creek
Kim Shuck

In Sonoma county there is a pear tree
Holding wall stones
Together with her roots
One suspended over the
Creek that undercuts both
She leans a heavy branch
Elbow down on the
Shoulder of the wall he
Keeps her mostly upright and the
Fruit the
Fruit could make your knees weak

Boxes
Heather Romero-Kornblum

How do we bury together

Children we didn't bring to fruition

The house we never built
gutters clogged before
having a chance to fill
Old age we may
not share with anyone

porches rockerless
sunsets unseen

How do I bury this life with you
I wanted so badly?

Random kitchenware
Cat-haired couch cushions
Shoeboxes of batteries
Nerve endings on our skin

All still pulse with life

gardens of Eden
beckon to be
fertilized
with my essence

How do I put myself
in your ground

when I still feel
electricity?

Duplex

Kelechi Ubozoh

—for James

Part 1. Today

Don't you know we're magic?

Ancestors in the algorithms answered with the divinity of you.
Handsome and humble.
Gentle strength.
Maintaining precious Black boy wonder and delight.
An innocence reserved for a few.

You taught me love and pain aren't mutually inclusive.
Healing childhood beliefs about love, worth, and belonging.

What if love was as easy as breathing?
What if it was fun?

Every day is a choice, and I choose you every day.

You love a turn of phrase and writing worlds that I hungrily devour.
You devour *me*.
Tracing constellations on your freckled brown skin.
Forever is easy with you.

Our interdimensional love mixtape spans space and time and includes:
A field of stars, X-men comic books, 90s hip hop, puns of all shapes and sizes, best friend inside jokes, intergalactic orgasms, alternative rock love songs, salmon sashimi, southern soul food, The Big Island's deep blue waves, crisp autumns in New York, vibrant summers in Wakanda, and our cat Atticus.

A love that is known in other lifetimes.
We've returned to each other.
A liberated/celebrated love

A be your weird goth/nerdy/neurospicy self 100% of the time love
Freedom.
The sweetest peach.

Earth Wind and Fire's "September" plays on our wedding day.
You whisper:
"Don't you know we're magic?"

Part 2. Yesterday and still somewhat today…

Collapse.
Stop the world. I want to get off.
Childhood best friend tumbled into the underworld
I want to join her.

Nightmares of her sweet face,
Scalding red hair,
Sugary laugh.

Life Machine continues, unfazed by this colossal loss.
Life Machine has bills, calendar invites, work and more work.

Frozen.
Dangerously decaying in the darkness.
Staring off in silence.
Breathing in the brokenness.

Grief makes other humans fidget,
Not you, my love.
You've known death a long time,
Consult with shadows,
Traversing quiet storms,
Bringing ancient wisdom to our home.

Nourished with bone marrow soup,
Wrapped in a thick heated blanket, a kiss upon my forehead.
Glasses gently removed, following another
insomnia binge-watch pain-soaked spree.

My pain doesn't drown you.
Somehow, you float.

Repeating the same phrases every day:

No, you aren't too much.
Did you eat anything today?
Let's get you some food.
No, I'm not mad at you.
Have you had any water?
Let's get you some water.
No, I don't regret marrying you. You are a wonderful partner.
What are you sorry for?
Please, stop apologizing.
Please take the space. I'm here for you. Always.
Have you had any water?
You're beautiful, yes, always—yes right now, yes in even your pajamas.
Have you gone outside today?
Let's get you some fresh air. Let's go for a walk.
    We don't have to go too far.
I love you.
You're my person. Yes, right now—especially now.
You're my soulmate.

Part 3. The beginning.

Walls high/fierce and tight. No one will get in this
    atrophied heart to destroy me again.
Broken engagements, psych ward grippy sock vacation,
    telenovela nightmares.
The one before scorched the earth inside my heart.

The last time was the last time, too much pain and paperwork.
Blackened and crisp, the charred heart remains reserved
    solely for chosen family.
Anyone else is just a good time guy, a passing delight, and a slick fuck.

I tell you:
"Look, I don't want anything serious. I'm *never* getting married
    and I'm *never* going to live with anyone."

Black honey brown eyes wide with other worldly knowing.
Cuz the ancestors whispered prophecies of our future love story—
alchemy of science and magic—all contingent upon how you
approach a *feral, rage-filled, bone-tired woman.*

You nod slowly/meet my eyes/gently squeeze my hand and
    in a tone wrapped in firm kindness say,
"it's okay, we can always get a Duplex."

Confession
Genny Lim

I am drawn to the faces of suicide bombers
The way free divers are drawn to the deep
The way yogis are drawn to caves
The way moths are drawn to flame
Something about the brute honesty
That knows no bounds
No lies or compromise
An intruder, in search of
Hidden mines, shadows
Where answers elude
And passions shape-shift
Into grenades
Then surrender to kisses

The terror of not knowing
What distance to cross or how far
One can fall without a net
Happens in a split second
With a finger on the pin
Frozen, reliving it all
The missed signs, the regrets
Stored in the empty pocket
Of displaced memory
Ready to erupt from the scar
Of the first and last kiss
Ready to expose, in sharp definition
What words can't unmask
In the feral orgasm of flesh
In the exultation
Of body and soul
Undifferentiated
Unbound

Seal Song
Gail Mitchell

Where Aurora rises
morning bursts forth
facets of jewels
echo the multi-hued light

Shades of chalcedony
awash in the limitless sea
staining winter
with thoughts of spring

Pushing past drifts
tides cannot mourn
or harbor resentments

We scan the waves for language
feeling the weight
of the restless herd

He picks the brightest words
for a bouquet
notices shells and a few sand dollars
strewn across the beach

It is a pleasant morning
open to possibility
creamy foam
washes over his wriggling toes
She lifts the shell to her heart
And dissolves

He turns sees her silken slip
of eternal blue
like froth on the waves

watches the pearls she was wearing
fall one at a time
onto the sandy floor

He follows the trail
slips his skin
returning to the sea
dives beneath the waves
scenting where she has gone

They float
one under the other
She measures distance
with each breath
drawn to his company

She places her secrets
in the coil of his spine
grows fur to match his coat
wraps herself in his furred warmth
sings the seal song

Shedding all traces of her past
Losing herself in his chorus
this change will push her
farthest from the shore

Cousin Kayla's Affair

Paul Corman Roberts

Oh, the relief when the rescue boats came! Mighty oar driven spectacles, as though they were creatures of salvation risen from the depths of the Marianas Trench come to save us from the doomed cruise liner as if on cue.

Of course, no one seemed to know why exactly the ship was doomed, or why these immaculate vehicles were summoned somehow separate from the lifeboats we were assured were deployable from the cruise liner proper. Neither did anyone seem to know or care where these deployable, onboard lifeboats were. All the passengers gathered to crowd the railings, with as many of their belongings as they could possibly hope to bring with them on these rescue crafts.

And as for us, the family/friends/community gathering that had somehow all come together on this voyage? What seemed to be on the edge of despair became a cause of hope and now perhaps cousin Kayla would call off her absurd fling with the cuttlefish who she had taken up with the moment of onboarding, and in this moment, we could leave that scandal in this brief reprieve.

And Kayla was there smiling with her cuttlefish and I immediately told her "no, the cephalopod is most assuredly restricted from the lifeboats" and instead of arguing or smirking she merely smiled her million dollar smile while Mr. Cuttlefish was suddenly quite absent (had he snuck aboard one of the lifeboats?)

Kayla's hair began wildly flowing about the deck of the sinking cruise liner and before I knew it Aunt Flossie, Uncle Bentley, Cousins Clarence and Grover and Tig, who had been preparing to board the lifeboats were suddenly ensnared in Kayla's flecked gray and white hair which was odd as her locks were absolute obsidian at the cruise beginning, but now it seemed as though aged streaks of salt were bolting through her hair which had now completely engulfed the deck, all our family and many other passengers whom had gathered to attempt to flee.

I don't know why I wasn't afraid. Mostly I was just exasperated with the whole state of affairs, but even one last, yearning look toward the glamorous rescue steeds showed them disappearing behind curtains of Kayla's all-encompassing empire of hair. It occurred to me that we wouldn't be likely to drown inside this place she had made for us.

Mostly I was just frustrated about how she always seemed to get her way no matter what, even on this damnable family retreat.

In The Company of Your Sweater
Karisma Rodriguez

I used to sleep in your sweater
And you said it made you feel special
Now it lies
Clumped and tied
I stare at it sometimes
But mostly look away
Convincing myself that I'll return it
Some day
Would it be too weird by then?
It already is now

But I'm a woman
And doesn't a woman
Have the right to treasure objects
That have been worn by souls
Touched by bodies
Especially their own
Don't they have a right
To keep what held them still
For just a little while

Trouble is
Your sweater isn't enough for me
Now that I'm awake

Your friend slept in my roommate's bed
And as they nestled into perfect niches
He said to her
One day we'll have a king-sized bed
I used my pillow to shield myself
From the sweetness
But it cut right through

And made me wish
You were more like him

I told you this and you said
It was a small goal to have
You would hold a prism to the light
Looking for dull clarity

You left your sweater on my bed
But this time I couldn't pretend
I wanted to smell your scent again
Truth dug its way into my heart
And I put it in the laundry instead

Each Morning
Chelsea Wills

one flowering quince blossom
each morning

I couldn't do it.
wake up, greet the wonder

get drunk on glowing green
run my fingers through the shiny soft
poison oak

instead I chased the wild
flapping my arms at the albino turkey

stop what you are doing
all that fresh green grass
only means you are older

I scowled at each daffodil
that beckoned change coming

kissed each tiny toenail
perfect pink pearls

and breathed in the perfume
of childhood
and pink yogurt

Coral Reaches, Jennifer Barone

Contributors

Adrian Arias is a Peruvian-American poet and multidisciplinary artist whose work explores memory, Indigenous ancestry, the body, and collective healing. Rooted in his Mochica heritage, his poetry bridges dreams, ritual, and lived experience, weaving personal and communal histories into lyrical narratives. Arias approaches language as a living space—one that invites reflection, resistance, and transformation. His poems often emerge in dialogue with visual art, performance, and public participation, creating intimate yet expansive encounters. Through his writing, Arias honors ancestral knowledge while confronting contemporary social and political realities, offering poetry as an act of visibility, resilience, and shared humanity. **adrianarias.com**

Al Averbach's work has appeared in *Poetalk, Ambush Review, Haight Ashbury Literary Journal, The Throwback, Bay Area Poets Seasonal Review,* the *Poets 11 Anthology (2008), The Gathering, The Guardsman,* and *Harm's Way* (chapbook). He's a multi-prizewinner in the Bay Area Poets Coalition and the Ina Coolbrith Circle contests, and was an editorial reader for *Poetalk*, Clara Hsu's Lao-Tzu Tao-te Ching: Translations and Infusions, Don Brennan's Extraordinary Pleasure, and The Poetry of Beth McDonald.

Jennifer Barone is an Italian-American poet and author of three poetry collections, including *Saporoso: Poems of Italian Food & Love*, Feather Press. A two-time winner of the SF Public Library's *Poets Eleven* contest for North Beach, where she resides. She hosts the *Voices From the Hill* podcast interviewing Bay Area authors for Telegraph Hill Books, and leads creative writing workshops that blend poetry, yoga, energy work, and Italian culture. She designs, teaches yoga (innerlotus.com), and delights in typing love poems for people on her vintage typewriter at special events. **jenniferbarone.wordpress.com**

Tom Batchelder is a poet and painter based in Sausalito, California. His background in expressive arts therapy, leadership coaching, and the fathering of two boys into thoughtful young men have shaped him. He says that he is healing himself through helping others and has a mission to "help a million kids to have parents that have passion and purpose at work and at home." **thomasbatchelder.com**

Bear sidesteps labels and boxes opting to live the song *Don't Fence Me In*, the David Byrne version please. Born with twelve fingers, he became a poet because somebody had to say it. He is writer, producer, DJ, streamer with the Bay Area music collective Soundwaves. He's never met a cheese or a dance floor he didn't like. **thebearcavesf.com**

DJ Benhaim is an emerging American poet born and raised in Chicago IL. His work interrogates memory, masculinity, cultural inheritance, and the fragile architecture of the heart, shaped in part by familial ties to South Africa. His poetry has appeared or is forthcoming in *Sheila-Na-Gig's Amplify Anthology*, *African Writer Magazine*, *The New Verse News*, and elsewhere. Writing where tenderness meets defiance, he explores love, grief, and emotional survival with urgency and precision. **@dariusjbenhaim**

Sara Biel is a poet and social worker living in Oakland, California. She is co-editor of the *Colossus Press* anthology series. Sara's chapbook, *Prescribed Burn* (2023), is available from Finishing Line Press. **@bielsara**

Jeffrey Bryant is a multiple Pushcart-nominated queer poet from Los Angeles, widely published in numerous journals and anthologies. His debut collection *The Catacombs of Vanished Lovers* is out now from Cherry Pie Press. **@jeffreybryant88**

Patrick Cahill's *The Machinery of Sleep* (Sixteen Rivers Press) appeared in 2020. A second collection, *If We are the Forest the Animals Dream*, also from Sixteen Rivers, appeared in 2025. His poems have twice won the Central Coast Writers Award. A cofounder and editor of *Ambush Review*, a San Francisco–based literary and arts journal, he was also a contributing editor for the anthology *Digging Our Poetic Roots: Poems from Sonoma County* (WordTemple Press). Cahill lives in San Francisco, where he volunteers with San Francisco Recreation and Parks in habitat restoration.

Paul Corman-Roberts was long listed for the 1993 SF Bay Guardian Poetry contest, winner of the 2010 Out Of Our Poetry Contest and short listed for the 2011 subTerrain fiction contest. He is the co-founder and co-producer of Collapse Press and its Zoomcast "The Friday Collapse" with his frequent collaborator Lynn Alexander. His most recent book is *19th Street Station, Volume 2* along with the forthcoming titles *Drink With The Coyotes* (a graphic novella) and a full length collection of poems *Love Poems from the Age of Late Stage Capitalism.* **cormanroberts.substack.com**

Brian Cronwall is a poet, playwright, and retired English professor from Kaua'i Community College in Hawai`i. His poetry has been awarded an Oscar Wilde Poetry Prize, been nominated for a Pushcart Prize, and been published in numerous journals and anthologies, including *Bamboo Ridge, Hawai`i Pacific Review, Santa Fe Literary Review, Carolina Quarterly, Poetry Ireland Review, Exit 13, Chiron Review,* and others.

Ruth Crossman is a Pushcart-nominated writer from Berkeley, California. She writes across a range of genres including poetry, flash fiction, memoir, and non-fiction. Her work has appeared in publications including *Litro, The Fabulist, Broke Ass Stuart,* and *Maximum Rock n' Roll.* **msruthcrossman.com**

Val DeBarra is a lesbian poet based in Dublin, Ireland. Their work moves through love, identity and human connection, shaped by queer experience and deep introspection. They write toward the tender and the undone, holding personal truth alongside emotions that ache into the universal, with an attention to intimacy and vulnerability. **@valvahurricane**

Justin Demeter is a queer/trans poet and painter who lives and loves in Oakland, CA. He has poems published by *New Words Press, Oxford University Press, Beyond the Veil Press, Passionfruit Review,* and *RogueAgent.* His special talents include climbing things, parallel parking, and catching falling objects. Justin peddles paperbacks on mental health for a living. **justindemeterart.com**

Natasha Dennerstein was born in Melbourne, Australia. She has an MFA from San Francisco State University. Natasha has had poetry published in many journals internationally, including The North American Review and Spoon River Poetry Review. She has had several poetry collections and chapbooks published including, most recently in 2024, the collection *Apps Poetica* from The Los Angeles Press and the chapbook *Caught in the Machine* from Be About It Press in Philadelphia. She lives in Oakland, California, where she is the editor of The Cherry Pie Press. She is a Fellow of the Lambda Literary Writer's Retreat. **natashadennerstein.com**

Victoria Dym is a graduate of Ringling Brothers Barnum and Bailey Clown College with a degree in Humility, a Bachelor of Arts, in Philosophy, from the University of Pittsburgh, and a Masters of Fine Arts, Creative Writing-Poetry from Carlow University. Class Clown, When the Walls Cave In, and The Hatchet Sun were published by Finishing Line Press in 2015, 2018 and 2023, respectively. Spontaneous was published by the West Florida Literary Federation in 2022. Victoria is an improv artist performing regularly in Tampa, Florida where she lives and teaches poetry, storytelling, improv and facilitates Laughter Yoga workshops.

Lourdes Figueroa is a queer Chicanx oral poet and poetry filmmaker based in the Bay Area, whose chapbooks, poetry film, and long verse explore memory, migration, and collective hxrstories. Their most recent work can be found in *Huizache 12*. A native of limbo nation, Lourdes continues to believe in your lung and your throat. **lourdesfigueroa.net**

Gianmaria Franchini is an Italian-American writer born in San Francisco, CA. He holds an MFA in Writing from the University of San Francisco and is currently completing a poetry collection, *Marzamemi*, about traveling from Palermo to Milan. His work reflects a life spent between cultures and landscapes, from Italian coasts to California shores. He is also a travel writer exploring the culture, people, and stories that shape life in Italy and the United States. **gianmariafranchini.com**

Alexandria Giardino is a bilingual creative force: she's an award-winning writer and translator, whose work includes the English-language translation of *My Life with Pablo Neruda*, by Matilde Urrutia, four children's book that have been translated into multiple languages, short fiction, and creative essays that have appeared in the various publications, such as *Marie Claire* (in Spanish), *the American Poetry Review*, and on air at KQED. When she's not writing, Alex is a somatic DJ, hosting dance parties in the US and Mexico. **alexgiardino.com**

Luisa M. Giulianetti is a Bay Area writer. Her debut collection, *Agrodolce* (Bordighera Press), was released in 2023. Her work has appeared in *CALYX*, *Rattle*, and *River Heron Review*. The daughter of Italian immigrants, Luisa is shaped by old-world experiences, stories, and lore. She retired from a 30+ year career at UC Berkeley and enjoys cooking, hiking, and exploring the expansive beauty of the place she calls home. Luisa credits her poetry group for keeping her energized and hopeful. **luisagiulianetti.com**

Hollie Hardy is the author of *Lions Like Us* (Red Light Lit Press) and *How to Take a Bullet: And Other Survival Poems* (Punk Hostage Press). She teaches private writing workshops online, and is the founder of Praxis Poetry: Weekly Prompts for Poets, and host of the long-running monthly reading series Saturday Night Special. Her work has been nominated for a Pushcart Prize and published in numerous anthologies and literary journals, including *Alchemy, Caesura, The Common, Fourteen Hills, Parley Lit, Passionfruit Review, Poetry Super Highway, The Quarter(ly), Synkronicity,* and elsewhere. **holliehardy.com**

Kary Hess, MFA, is an artist exploring how languages of place contour our lived experience. She's the author of *1912, Poems of Time, Place, and Memory,* creator of the *SparkTarot®* Deck and Guidebook, and an independent film producer. She's also the director of the Petaluma Poetry Walk, the editor of its annual anthology, and a regular contributor to the *Pacific Sun, North Bay Bohemian* and *North Bay Magazine* where she writes about arts and culture. Her work asks the questions: "Are we made of place? Who would we be if we spoke the languages of our landscapes?" **karyhess.com**

E.K. Keith poet and librarian, has poetry published in journals and anthologies locally, nationally, internationally, and digitally. Her first book, *Ordinary Villains,* is available from Black Lawrence Press. A labor of love supported by San Francisco Public Library, E.K. organizes and hosts the 21st Annual Poems Under the Dome, San Francisco's open mic celebration of poetry month, happening again April 24, 2026 from 5:30-8pm inside San Francisco's City Hall. See you there!

Lam Khong was born in Saigon, Vietnam in 1972 during the war, and escaped by boat in 1980. In America, he learned English, and also relied on drawing to communicate and heal. He has exhibited in Berkeley, Boston, Denver, Florida, New York, Rome and Santa Fe. His art has been published in poetry books including *Heroic Virtue, Ruah,* and *Saporoso, Poems of Italian Food & Love* (Feather Press). He has written a memoir *Blue Song* about his mother who risked her life to smuggle her children out of Vietnam. He has a BFA, College of Santa Fe and an MFA from American University.

Len Kuntz is a writer from Washington State and the author of six books, most recently, *Things I Can't Even Tell Myself,* out from Ravenna Press. You can find more of his writing at **lenkuntz.blogspot.com**

Char Lacsina is a poet based in San Francisco. She has been writing since she was twelve, filling notebooks with feelings she didn't yet know how to name. Her work explores love, longing, and the afterlife of heartbreak—the moments that stay with us long after the story has ended. When she isn't writing, she works at the intersection of technology and social impact, and lives with her doodle, Crosby, who reminds her to pause between poems. **@charlacsina**

Maggie La Rochelle is a poet and farmer. She lives with her family in Sonoma, CA where she and her husband operate Sunray Farm, a small organic vegetable farm. She studied English at UC San Diego where she published poems in local zines and student journals before going on to careers in academia and then farming. She is a proud mom and seeker of new growth and creative experiences.

Brittiany Lema is a poet whose work explores love as a force of fracture and repair. Drawing from lived experience, mythic resonance, and emotional immediacy, her poems move through devotion, longing, grief, desire, and the quiet aftermaths that follow intimacy. She is especially interested in the places where tenderness meets survival, where the body remembers what the heart tries to forget. **@brittianylema**

Lynn Light is a healer, acupuncturist, and accidental poet. Rooted in the healing arts, she engages humans where spirit meets skin. A Gemini who delights in wordplay, she welcomes the occasional poem that insists on being born. Lynn loves dancing with vinyl nerds and epic sound systems, making collage art, and camping near sparkling bodies of water. She believes healing and poetry share a common language: presence, being seen, and feeling it all. This marks her first published poem birthing. **clearpathwayshealth.com**

Genny Lim is the ninth San Francisco Poet Laureate of San Francisco and a former San Jazz Poet Laureate, She is author of five poetry collections and *Island: Poetry and History of Chinese Immigrants on Angel Island*, winner of the American Book Award, and the recipient of two lifetime achievement awards from PEN Oakland and city of Berkeley. **gennylim.ddns.net**

Candace Loheed, based in San Francisco since the early seventies, was born in Springfield, Vermont, educated at Purdue University, SFMOMA, Revere Academy, San Francisco Art institute. She spent

20 years as ceramic jewelry designer and manufacturer of Parrot Pearls, and Ruby Z with Bean Finneran in San Francisco. Shown internationally in galleries, specialty shops, aquariums, museums, including Smithsonian. Loheed also participated in Alan Finneran's Soon 3, the avant guard theater company. She has been painting, writing, making new jewelry and ceramics while organizing shows and events for Orangeland Gallery which she founded in 2005. **orangelandgallery.com**

Anne Marie Wenzel was born in San Francisco and earned a master's degree in economics from San Francisco State University. She has studied creative writing through Berkeley's Left Margin Lit, and Stanford Continuing Studies, where she earned a certificate in Novel Writing. Her poetry has been published in *Humble Pie, the California Writer's Club 2022 Literary Review,* and *Faltzone: Detachment.* She lives on the San Francisco Peninsula. **annemariewenzel.com**

M.G. Martin is the author of *U U O U* (Cyberwit, 2020) and *One For None* (Ink., 2010). He has performed on stages in San Francisco, Oakland, Los Angeles, San Diego, Portland, Boston, New York City, Seoul, and Honolulu. His poems have appeared in *Tinfish*, *ZYZZYVA*, *Juked*, *PANK*, and *Bamboo Ridge*, among others. M.G. has also led writing workshops for the Red Cross, the Hawaii Council for the Humanities, and was a W.S. Merwin Creative Teaching Fellow. **mgmartin.ink**

Gail Mitchell has always drawn on it to map the internal terrain and make sense of the external world. She draws on the word to investigate life and death - traversing a language that leaves her spellbound. Words are Gail's foundation and making a poem is part resistance, part fury. Emmett Till sits under her breast- bone. History shatters her heart. And poverty is a scathing rebuke, so she writes. It is the only way she can make sense of humanity being inhumane. Ms. Mitchell received her BA and MFA in Creative Writing from San Francisco State University. *Bone Songs* was published by Taurean Horn Press in 1999. Gail Mitchell is a poet living in San Francisco.

K.R. Morrison Since the pandemic, K.R. Morrison has been searching for mermaids in a sea town in Southern California, often returning to the Bay Area for her poetry nests and to play drums for two all-female fronted rock bands – Harriot and Unicröne. Morrison is a three-time Pushcart Nominee for her poems, *Her Altar, Ode to Grief,* and *i remember,* and her first poetry collection *Cauldrons* was published by Paper Press in July, 2021. When she's not submerging in poetry, K.R. Morrison is a writing workshop facilitator, a tarot reader, and a natal chart intuitive reader. **@k.r.morrisonpoet**

Peggy Morrison is a California poet grateful for the San Francisco Bay Area's fertile literary community. Her poetry chapbook, *Mom Says,* celebrates voice as a living embodiment of culture and history. Her poems are published in several journals and anthologies, and she is co-editor of the anthologies *Day Without Art* (Pandemonium Press) and *Colossus: Body* (Colossus Press). Peggy has been honored to read in international poetry festivals in Cuba and Kenya. When not reading or writing poetry, Peggy might be found tending her vegetable garden, hiking in the redwoods, or dancing.

Elisabeth Nails is a poet, social worker and program designer with over 15 years of experience using the arts as a catalyst for healing, youth development, and cross-system collaboration. She leads Creative Wellbeing at the Los Angeles County Department of Arts and Culture, an award-winning initiative serving more than 12,000 youth and 20,000 adults annually across child welfare, mental health, foster care, and justice systems. Her work centers restorative practice, trauma-informed design, and equitable access to healing-centered care. She is Co-Chair of the Los Angeles Suicide Prevention Network's Youth Advisory Board and co-founder of Typewriters Anonymous. **typewritersanonymous.com**

Phillip T. Nails is a lovechild born at the base of Mt. Diablo in Northern California. He was first put in touch with the muse when some Beat poets visited his high school at it was then, Nails decided he wanted to be a performance poet. Decades later, Nails continues in the lineage of The Beats and has studied with poets and performance artists Brett Bevell, Tim Miller, Mary Overlie and Guillermo Gómez-Peña. It is in these veins that Nails explores poetry and performance. **typewritersanonymous.com**

Michelle Patton received an MFA in Creative Writing from California State University, Fresno. She won the Ernesto Trejo Award for poetry in 2003 and was nominated for a Pushcart Prize. Her poems have been published in Rattle, The Atlanta Review, Southern Poetry Review, Calyx, Zyzzyva, Prairie Schooner, Cutbank, and others. She teaches English at Fresno City College.

Egan Reeve is an Irish queer poet and community organiser who splits their time between Cork City and their rural hometown. A graduate of UCC, they are currently the guest editor of several local publications, and co-founded a queer open mic night - Litreacha. **@eganreeve**

Karisma Rodriguez has been writing poetry and prose since age 8. Her work has been published in a New York Times bestselling anthology and a textbook on intercultural communication, among various other literary journals. She holds a B.A. in English with a Creative Writing Concentration in Poetry from UCLA. **karismarodriguez.com**

Heather Romero-Kornblum is a former academic researcher, returning to poetry after several near-death experiences due to Long Covid. She captures the crumbling of her marriage following her near-death experiences in *I'M NOT OVER YOU* – the 2025 Four Feathers Press Chapbook Contest winner. She is published in multiple anthologies and journals including *The Zest of the Lemon, Plague 2020, Women Who Submit 'This Makes up the Sky'* and *'Accolades,' LA Art News Poet's Place, Quiet Lightning's 'Sparkle and Blink,' Four Feathers Press* monthly anthologies, and on the ZZyZx WriterZ podcast. She also hosts the weekly Poetic Problems workshop. **heatherkornbooks.com**

Elisa Salasin is a poet and educator based in Berkeley, CA. She has poetry, essays, and photography published in *The Los Angeles Press, Rising Phoenix Review, always electric,* SF Public Library Poem of the Day, *sPARKLE & bLINK, CounterPunch,* and the Bay Area Writing Project's Digital Paper. She is an editor for *Colossus Press*. Her first chapbook, *She Watches Wild Horses,* was published in 2023 by Finishing Line Press. **@elisa_sal**

Shizue Seigel is a Japanese American writer and artist based in San Francisco. As director of Write Now! SF Bay, she supports writers and artist of color through workshops, events and publications. She's a VONA/Voices fellow and Jefferson Award recipient whose ninth book, *Courting A Man Who Doesn't Talk,* was published in 2024. **writenowsf.com** & **shizueseigel.com**

Elizabeth Shanaz is a New York based writer and poet with an extensive body of work focused on motifs related to millennial consciousness, Muslim womanhood, and diasporic memory. She was nominated three times for the 2026 Best of the Net in the category of poetry, and won third place in the 2026 Humans of the World Winter Poetry Prize. She currently holds a literary arts residency at Barzakh Café in Brooklyn, New York. **@lizzieshanaz**

Maw Shein Win's most recent full-length poetry collection is *Percussing the Thinking Jar* (Omnidawn, 2024), and her previous collection is *Storage Unit for the Spirit House* (Omnidawn, 2020). She teaches poetry in the MFA Program at the University of San Francisco and at Saint Mary's College of California. **mawsheinwin.com**

Kim Shuck likes dancing barefoot on her frosty porch just before dawn. Shuck is a visual artist and poet from San Francisco and served as the 7th Poet Laureate of that city. There have been awards, degrees, publications and other literary lint. Kim's latest full length solo book, as of this writing, is *Pick a Garnet to Sleep In*.

James J. Siegel is the author of the poetry collections *The God of San Francisco* and *How Ghosts Travel*. He is the host and curator of the monthly Literary Speakeasy show at Martuni's piano bar in San Francisco. His poems have been featured in several journals and anthologies, including Foglifter, the Cortland Review, Borderlands: Texas Poetry Review, and more. **@jamessiegelpoet**

Jonathan Siegel Love is what brought me to poetry, and it is in love…I continue to find my greatest cause to write. Love can make any wordless fool a Poet. And a Poet…a wordless fool. **jonathan-siegel-n0or.squarespace.com**

Norma Smith was born in Detroit and grew up in Fresno, California. She has lived in the San Francisco Bay Area for most of her life as a writer, editor, social researcher, educator, and event and conference organizer. She has also worked as a journalist and translator-interpreter and now organizes online and in-person writing workshops. Her work has been published in literary, scholarly, and political journals. She has been a featured reader at Lyrics & Dirges, Quiet Lightning, La Palabra Musical, and other Bay Area reading series. **normasmithwriter.com**

Richard Stimac lives in the St. Louis, Missouri (USA) area. He has published a poetry book *Bricolage* (Spartan Press), two poetry chapbooks, and one flash fiction chapbook. In his work, Richard explores time and memory through the landscape and humanscape of the St. Louis region. He invites you to follow his poetry Facebook page: "Richard Stimac poet".

Kelechi Ubozoh is a Nigerian-American writer and mental health advocate who blends realities of trauma, race, mental health, and healing into her writing. She co-authored *We've Been Too Patient* with L.D. Green, now available as an audiobook, amplifying marginalized voices in mental health. Her work has been featured in *Argot Magazine, Multiplicity, Endangered Species, Enduring Values, Essential Truths, Trauma, Tresses, & Truth: Untangling Our Hair Through Personal Narrative*, and *When We Exhale.* She co-hosts the Bay Area reading series MoonDrop Productions with Cassandra Dallett. Kelechi has received a Pushcart Prize nomination. **kelechiubozoh.com.**

Joseph Voth writes from California's Central Valley where he also teaches for the English Department at Fresno City College. His first book of poetry, *Living with Noise*, was published by NorthShore Press.

Chelsea Wills born 1984. She is an artist and writer based in Northern California. She released her debut chapbook, *The Home of Milk* (2024) with Bottlecap Press. Her writing and art can be found across the internet, most recently at Recenter Journal, Her art has been shown at Yerba Buena Center for the Arts, San Jose Museum of Art, Kala Art Institute, and more. She was the Anne Marie Oomen Fellow at Poetry Forge. **chelseawills.com**

Acknowledgements

Thank you to all of the contributors who trusted me with their poems, their hearts, their truths. This book exists because of your courage and generosity.

Thank you to Jennifer Barone—poet, designer, collaborator, soul-sister—for your expert creative direction and for bringing this book to life with vision and care.

Thank you to the 30/30 poets, the Burns Night crew, Hollie Hardy, Justin Demeter, Kim Shuck, Phillip & Elisabeth Nails, Jon Siegel, Afi Ayanna, Lynn Light, Kyle Knobel, Kary Hess & the Petaluma Poetry Walk, and the many poets to whom I give my heart. You are my creative family. You remind me why this matters.

FEATHER PRESS

About Feather Press

Feather Press is an independent literary press dedicated to uplifting the voices of local poets, writers, and artists. We believe in creative abundance—that every individual carries a deep well of story, history, and lineage waiting to be expressed. Guided by a commitment to cultural and racial diversity, we support both emerging and established voices with care and intention.

Through single-author poetry collections, the *Tender Hearts Club* anthology series, and community gatherings, Feather Press creates space for connection, celebration, and the shared power of story. We publish work that is honest, radiant, and real—work that refuses to shrink in a world asking us to harden.

To learn more about our publications and upcoming events, visit **featherpressbooks.wordpress.com**

About the Editor

Ingrid Keir is the founder of Feather Press, a poet and a longtime curator of the literary community. She has spent years creating spaces for writers to gather and grow—through workshops, readings, and events that center creative abundance and intentional care. *Tender Hearts Club* is her ongoing devotion to lifting up love as a force, a practice, and a way forward. She lives in Petaluma, CA with her daughter.

You can find out more about her at **ingridkeir.com**

Love is real.
Welcome to the love parade.

www.ingramcontent.com/pod-product-compliance
Lightning Source LLC
Chambersburg PA
CBHW021639080526
44584CB00015BA/1612